BOSTON COMMON PRESS
Brookline, Massachusetts

1998

Boston Common Press
17 Station Street
Brookline, Massachusetts 02146

ISBN 0-936184-25-6
Library of Congress Cataloging-in-Publication Data
The Editors of *Cook's Illustrated*
    How to grill: An illustrated step-by-step guide to cooking steaks, chops, burgers, seafood, chicken, and vegetables outdoors/The Editors of *Cook's Illustrated*
1st ed.

    Includes 45 recipes and 41 illustrations
    ISBN 0-936184-25-6 (hardback): $14.95
    I. Cooking. I. Title
1998

Manufactured in the United States of America

Distributed by Boston Common Press, 17 Station Street, Brookline, MA 02146.

Cover and text design: Amy Klee
Recipe development: Melissa Hamilton
Series Editor: Jack Bishop

HOW TO GRILL

An illustrated step-by-step guide to
cooking steaks, chops, burgers, seafood,
chicken, and vegetables outdoors.

THE COOK'S ILLUSTRATED LIBRARY

Illustrations by John Burgoyne

CONTENTS

introduction

Grilling and barbecue are everyman's cuisine and they are uniquely American. Yet most grilled foods are often inedible. I've had too much charred-on-the-outside, raw-on-the-inside chicken, steak, and fish. And much of that food I cooked myself. The editors of *Cook's* wanted to discover how to grill foods simply and perfectly. Hence this modest but well-researched volume that covers steaks, burgers, pork tenderloin, pork chops, lamb chops, chicken, fish steaks, shellfish, and vegetables. Each method is thoroughly tested to find the ideal blend of technique and practicality.

We start with the basics—the choice of fuel and equipment. Testing revealed that gas grills are inferior to kettle-style charcoal grills, which produce more heat and hold plenty of fuel. Two different levels of fire are also important so that foods can be quickly seared and then set over lower heat to cook through. Using cheap aluminum pans to cover foods during cooking was superior to using a grill cover, which often imparts an off flavor.

You will find many of the conclusions in this book surprising. We recommend a quick brine as a good preparation method for both shrimp and chicken. We tested different cuts of chops and found that some inferior and less expensive cuts actually have better flavor. We also found that marinating thin tuna steaks in olive oil keeps them from drying out over a hot fire.

This is only one volume in a series that includes *How to Make a Pie, How to Make an American Layer Cake, How to Stir-Fry, How to Make Ice Cream, How to Make Pizza, How to Make Holiday Desserts, How to Make Pasta Sauces,* and *How to Make Salad.* Many other titles in this series will soon be available. To order other books, call (800) 611-0759. We also publish *Cook's Illustrated,* a bimonthly publication about American home cooking. For a free trial copy of *Cook's,* call (800) 526-8442.

Christopher P. Kimball
Publisher and Editor
Cook's Illustrated

chapter one

GRILLING
BASICS

GRILLING IS THE QUICK-COOKING (OR SEAR-
ing) of foods over an open fire. Grilled
foods are fairly thin so that they can cook
through over a hot fire without causing the
exterior to char. Larger cuts, such as roasts or whole birds,
can be cooked over an open fire, but they require lower
cooking temperatures and longer cooking times, as well as
the use of indirect heat and the cover. Although many cooks
call this grilling, a turkey or brisket is technically barbecued
or grill-roasted. True grilling, which is the subject of this
book, is hotter and faster.

Grilling is not a science. Fire is a living, changing entity

8

that requires constant attention and rapid response to current conditions. Gas grills deliver consistent results but often sacrifice intensity in the process. (For information on using a gas grill, *see* page 20.) Charcoal fires do a better job of searing and browning. We also find that charcoal-grilled foods taste better. Adding up all the pluses and minuses, we think that working with a live charcoal fire is worth the effort.

All the recipes in this book were tested on a kettle-style grill using hardwood lump charcoal (*see* figure 1, page 14). During the hundreds of hours we spent cooking outdoors to produce this book, we developed the following guidelines for optimum results when grilling.

⠞ USE A KETTLE GRILL. We find that a round kettle-style grill is the best all-purpose choice for outdoor cooking. The large cooking grate (usually at least 16 inches across and often as much as 22 inches in diameter) allows you to prepare a good amount of food at one time. Also, the deep kettle holds a lot of charcoal so you can build a big, hot fire.

⠞ USE ENOUGH CHARCOAL. Many cooks stint on the fuel when grilling and never get the temperature high enough. There's no point spending $30 on steaks and then steaming them over an inadequate fire. The size of your grill, the amount of food being cooked, and the desired intensity of the fire are all factors in deciding how much charcoal to use. In the end, you want a fire that is slightly larger than the space on the cooking grate occupied by food. Remember that you can always let the fire die down a bit if the heat is too intense. It's possible to add more charcoal if the fire is too weak, but this involves lifting up the hot cooking grate, which is awkward and inconvenient.

For most jobs, we light one chimney full of charcoal. When the coals are well lit and covered with gray ash, we dump them on the grill bottom and add the rest of the charcoal (*see* figure 2, page 15). Five pounds of charcoal (or more when a blazing hot fire is needed for cooking steaks) is not an unreasonable amount.

:: BUILD THE RIGHT KIND OF FIRE. There are two basic types of charcoal fires you can build in a grill. When the coals are lit, they may be spread out evenly across the bottom of the grill (*see* figure 3, page 15). A single-level fire delivers even heat across the cooking grate, usually at a moderate temperature because the coals are fairly distant from the cooking grate. We cook vegetables and shrimp over this kind of fire.

A second option, one that we employ in most instances, is a two-level fire. Once the coals are lit, some of the coals should be raked off the pile and spread out in a single layer across half the grill bottom. The remaining coals stay piled up on the other side of the grill so that they are closer to the cooking grate (*see* figure 4, page 16).

There are several advantages to a two-level fire. The heat above the pile of coals is quite hot, perfect for searing. The heat above the single layer of coals is less intense, perfect for cooking thicker foods once they are well browned. This cooler part of the fire also comes in handy if flames engulf food. Simply drag the food to the cooler part of the grill and the fire will usually subside.

▪▪ TAKE THE FIRE'S TEMPERATURE. Different foods require different heat intensities. To gauge the temperature of the fire, hold your hand 5 inches above the cooking grate and use the timing in figure 5 on page 17 to determine the heat level. If the fire is not hot enough, add more charcoal. If the fire is too hot, wait for the heat to dissipate a bit.

▪▪ GET THE RIGHT TOOLS. Many grill manufacturers produce sets of long-handled tools for use with the grill. We prefer less expensive, sturdier tools such as a long-handled fork, a spring-loaded tongs, a dogleg metal spatula, a paintbrush, and a wire brush for cleaning the grill (*see* figure 8, page 19). Some grill grids have hinged sections that make it much easier to add charcoal to the fire during cooking (*see* figure 6, page 18). If you have a choice, buy a grill with this feature.

▋▋ DON'T USE THE COVER. Over time, soot and resinous compounds can build up on the inside of a kettle grill cover. For this reason, we don't use the cover when grilling since we find that the cover often imparts a slightly "off" taste, which we can best described as resembling the odor of stale smoke. We prefer to use a disposable aluminum roasting or pie pan to cover foods that require some buildup of heat to cook them through.

▋▋ THICKER IS OFTEN BETTER. In general, moderately thick steaks, fish fillets, and chops are easier to grill because they will be well seared by the time the inside is properly cooked. Very thin steaks, chops, and fish fillets are harder to keep moist, especially if you like a crisp exterior. When shopping, you may need to ask the butcher or fishmonger to cut meat or fish to fit your needs.

▋▋ COOKING TIMES ARE ESTIMATES. Cooking over a live fire is not like cooking in a precisely calibrated oven. Be prepared to adjust timing, especially if grilling in cool or windy weather. An instant-read thermometer or taking the meat off the grill and peeking with the tip of a knife are the best ways of telling when food is cooked to your liking.

■■ WE LIKE IT RARE. We find that beef, pork, and fish are more flavorful and juicier when cooked short of well done, either rare, medium-rare, or medium, depending on the item in question. If you are worried about killing possible bacteria, you should cook all meat and seafood to an internal temperature of at least 160 degrees. Of course, chicken must be well done in all cases.

Figure 1.

Commonly available fuels include (clockwise from top right), charcoal briquettes, lump hardwood charcoal, wood chips, and hardwood logs. We recommend hardwood charcoal; it burns hotter and cleaner than standard briquettes. If you want to add smokiness, consider adding some hardwood logs or wood chunks to the fire. If using wood chips, wrap them in aluminum foil, poke some holes in the foil, and put the packet directly on the coals.

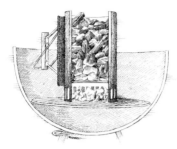

Figure 2.

Our favorite way to start a charcoal fire is with a flue starter, also
known as a chimney starter. To use this simple device, fill the
bottom section with crumpled newspaper, set the flue on the grill
grate, and fill the top with charcoal. When you light the newspaper,
flames will shoot up through the charcoal, igniting it. When the
coals are well lit and covered with a layer of gray ash, dump them
onto the charcoal grate, and add the rest of the charcoal. Continue
heating until all the coals are gray.

Figure 3.

At this point, the coals can be arranged in an even layer to create
a single-level fire. This kind of fire delivers even heat and is best
for quick searing at a moderate temperature.

15

Figure 4.
*A two-level fire permits searing over very hot coals and slower
cooking over medium coals to cook through thicker cuts. To build
a two-level fire, spread some of the lit coals in a single layer over
half the grill. Leave the remaining coals in a pile that rises to
within 2 or 2½ inches of the cooking grate.*

16

Figure 5.
Once the coals have been spread out in the bottom of the grill,
put the cooking grate in place, and put the cover on for 5 minutes
to heat up the grate. Before cooking, determine the intensity of
the fire by holding your hand 5 inches above the cooking grate.
When the fire is hot, you should be able to keep your hand in
place for no more than 2 seconds. For a medium-hot fire, the time
extends to 3 or 4 seconds; for a medium fire, 5 or 6 seconds; and
for a medium-low fire, 7 seconds.

17

Figure 6.
If the fire is not hot enough, add more charcoal. Some grills come
with a hinged cooking grate that makes it easier to add charcoal
or move coals around when cooking.

Figure 7.
If the cooking grate is not hinged, use a pair of fire-resistant
gloves to lift it off the grill, and then add more charcoal.

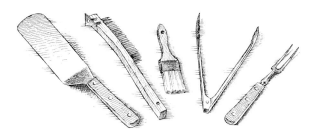

Figure 8.

*We find the following tools useful when grilling. From left, a dogleg
spatula for lifting foods off the grill, a wire brush for cleaning the
grill grate, a paintbrush for brushing on sauces and marinades,
spring-loaded tongs, and a long-handled fork for turning foods.*

Figure 9.

*If foods start to flame, pull them to the cooler part of the grill
(an advantage of working with a two-level fire) or use a squirt
bottle to douse the flames with water.*

19

NOTES ON USING A GAS GRILL

Gas grills are increasing in popularity and the reasons are clear—the fire is easy to light and control. But while there are some $3,000 units that can produce a blazing hot fire, most gas grills cannot approach the heat level of a good hot charcoal fire. If you want a truly crisp crust on a steak, gas is not going to deliver the same results as charcoal. However, for foods that require cooler fires, such as vegetables or shrimp, the results on a gas grill will be fine.

The recipe instructions in this book give the proper heat level, which is determined by holding your hand five inches off the cooking grate (*see* figure 5, page 17). If using a gas grill, adjust the dials to produce the correct temperature.

Most gas grills come with two temperature controls, each regulating a separate burner. You can use the dials to change the heat level on the entire grill, turning the heat from high to medium once food has been seared. The dials can also be manipulated to create two heat levels on the cooking surface at the same time. For instance, you may set one burner at high for searing and set the other at medium to cook foods through or to have a place to move foods if they ignite.

One final note about gas grills. Unlike charcoal grills, the inside of the cover stays fairly clean. Since there is no buildup of resinous smoke, the grill cover (rather than a disposable aluminum pan) can be used.

Figure 10.
*We wish propane tanks
had a gauge that would
register the gas level. You
can get an idea of how
much gas is left in the
tank by using this trick.
Pour a cup or so of boiling
water over the tank.*

Figure 11.
*Feel the metal with your
hand. Where the water
has succeeded in warm-
ing the tank, it is empty;
where the tank remains
cool to the touch, there is
still propane inside.*

chapter two

GRILLED STEAKS & BURGERS

THE KEY TO COOKING STEAKS PROPERLY IS high heat. For an all-over seared crust, a very hot charcoal fire is a must. The coals must come within 2½ inches of the cooking grate. While this intense heat is needed to produce the crisp crust we like, it will burn the exterior of the steak before it is cooked through. We found that making a two-level fire (with coals piled high on one side and spread out on the other side of the grill) is necessary. After a quick searing over the very hot part of the fire, we move the steaks over the single layer of coals to cook through.

This system acts as insurance against bonfires; at the

first sign of a flare-up, slide the steak to the cooler part of the grill. A two-level fire also solves the problem of cooking a porterhouse or T-bone steak that contains delicate tenderloin meat on one side of the bone and strip on the other side. Simply position these steaks so that the strip is over the hotter fire and the tenderloin is over the cooler fire.

For all cuts of steak, look for meat that has a bright, lively color. Beef normally ranges from pink to red, but dark meat probably indicates an older, tougher animal. The external fat as well as the fat that runs through the meat (called intramuscular fat or marbling) should be as white as possible. The marbling should be smooth and fine, running through the meat, and not in clumps. Stay away from packaged steaks that show a lot of red juice (known as "purge"). The purge may indicate a bad freezing job, and the steaks will be dry and cottony.

Grilling hamburgers requires a different technique. Their high fat content makes burgers particularly susceptible to flare-ups, but you still need enough heat to generate a good crust. The solution is a fire made of a single layer of coals. The heat is even but not overly intense.

Chuck is the best choice of meat for burgers. It has a robust, beefy flavor that other cuts do not. If you like, ask your butcher to grind a chuck roast to order or do it yourself in a food processor.

NOTES ON CUTS OF BEEF FOR STEAK

There are nine primal cuts of beef sold at the wholesale level. A butcher will trim these primal cuts into retail cuts. Steaks generally come from the following parts of the cow.

SHOULDER/CHUCK: Often labled London broil, steaks from this region are boneless and consist of a single muscle. Buy a shoulder steak that is ½ to 2 pounds and slice it thin on the bias. We find that shoulder steaks offer the best value for cost-conscious shoppers.

RIB: Rib, rib eye, or Delmonico steaks can be cut with or without the bone. They are tender and have a beefy flavor.

SHORT LOIN: Our favorite steak, the strip or top loin, is cut from this region. The tenderloin and filet mignon also come from the short loin, but we find them overly tender. The T-bone and porterhouse contain a nice balance of chewy strip and buttery tenderloin.

SIRLOIN: Sometimes labled London broil, these steaks are tougher than short loin steaks and not as highly prized.

ROUND: Steaks cut from the round (most often called London broil steaks) are boneless and quite lean. We find them dry and chewy and generally avoid them.

FLANK: The tender, boneless, single-muscle steak from the flank is often sold as London broil. It is fairly thin (no more than an inch thick) and weighs 1½ to 2 pounds. Like shoulder steaks, slice this cut on the bias for serving.

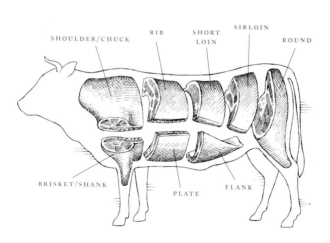

DIAGRAM NO. I

25

Grilled Strip Steak

➤ **NOTE:** *Strip steaks (also called top loin), either on or off the bone, are our first choice for grilling individual steaks. You may also use rib eye steaks. (See figures 12 and 13, pages 27 and 28, for descriptions of each steak.) This recipe yields four large servings. If you would rather limit portions to 8 ounces, grill two 1-pound steaks, slice them, and then serve each person half a steak. Serve as is or with one of the compound butters on page 38.*

4   **strip steaks with or without bone,**
     1¼ to 1½ inches thick (12 to 16 ounces each)
     Salt and ground black pepper

▮▮ **INSTRUCTIONS:**

1. Build a two-level fire (*see* figure 4, page 16). Set grill rack in place, cover grill with lid, and let rack heat up, about 5 minutes.

2. Sprinkle both sides of each steak with salt and pepper to taste. Grill, uncovered, over very hot fire until well browned on one side, 2 to 3 minutes. Turn each steak; grill until well browned on second side, 2 to 3 minutes. (If steaks start to flame, pull them to cooler part of grill or extinguish flames.)

3. Once steaks are well browned on both sides, slide each one to cooler part of grill. Continue grilling over medium fire to desired doneness, 5 to 6 minutes more for rare (120 degrees on instant-read thermometer), 6 to 7 minutes for medium-rare on the rare side (125 degrees), 7 to 8 minutes for medium-rare on the medium side (130 degrees), or 8 to 9 minutes for medium (135 to 140 degrees). Let steaks rest 5 minutes, then serve immediately.

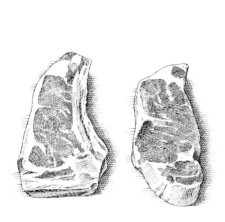

Figure 12.
Strip steak (also called shell, New York strip, or top loin) is our favorite cut for grilling. It is moderately chewy with a noticeable grain. The flavor is excellent, with slightly less fat than rib. The strip steak on the left is on the bone; the strip steak on the right is off the bone.

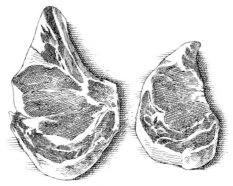

Figure 13.

We also like rib eye (also called rib) steaks on the grill. They are
very tender and smooth textured. The distinctive beefy taste is
robust and rich, with pockets of fat in the meat. The rib eye on
the left is on the bone; the rib eye on the right is off the bone.

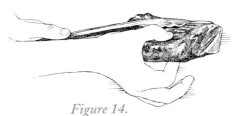

Figure 14.

There are two ways to tell when a steak is properly cooked.
To judge doneness by texture, pick up the steak and compare the
texture to that of your hand. A rare steak will approximate the
soft, squishy feel of the skin between your thumb and forefinger.
Make a fist and do the same to give the springy feel of medium,
or touch the tip of your nose for well done.

28

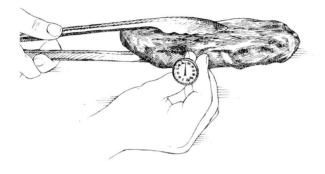

Figure 15.

An instant-read thermometer can be slid sideways into a steak to judge doneness. Push the tip of the thermometer through the edge of the steak and make sure that most of the shaft is embedded in the meat and not touching any bone. Pull the steak off the grill when it registers 120 degrees for rare; 125 to 130 degrees for medium-rare; 135 to 140 degrees for medium.

Grilled Porterhouse or T-Bone Steak

➤ **N O T E :** *Both the porterhouse and T-bone combine pieces of the strip and tenderloin. These steaks are so large it's best to have the butcher cut them thick (about 1½ inches) and let each steak serve two people. Serve as is or top with a dollop of compound butter (see recipes on page 38) as soon as the steaks come off the grill.*

   2   porterhouse or T-bone steaks, each 1½ inches
         thick (about 3½ pounds total)
         Salt and ground black pepper

I N S T R U C T I O N S :

1. Build a two-level fire (*see* figure 4, page 16). Set grill rack in place, cover grill with lid, and let rack heat up, about 5 minutes.

2. Meanwhile, sprinkle both sides of each steak with salt and pepper to taste. Position steaks so that strip pieces are over hottest part of fire and tenderloin pieces are over cooler part of fire (*see* figure 17, page 33). Grill, uncovered, until well browned on one side, 2 to 3 minutes. Turn each steak; grill until well browned on second side, 2 to 3 minutes. (If steaks start to flame, pull them to cooler part of grill or extinguish flames.)

3. Once steaks are well browned on both sides, slide each one to cooler part of grill. Continue grilling over medium fire to

3 0

desired doneness, 5 to 6 minutes more for rare (120 degrees on instant-read thermometer), 6 to 7 minutes for medium-rare on the rare side (125 degrees), 7 to 8 minutes for medium-rare on the medium side (130 degrees), or 8 to 9 minutes for medium (135 to 140 degrees). Let steaks rest 5 minutes, cut off strip and tenderloin pieces and slice them each crosswise about ⅓ inch thick (*see* figures 18–20, pages 34 and 35). Serve immediately.

VARIATION:

Tuscan Steak with Lemon and Olive Oil

Called *bistecca Fiorentina*, this dish is traditionally made with T-bone steak.

Rub each steak with 2 tablespoons extra-virgin olive oil and sprinkle with salt and pepper to taste. Grill as directed. Serve steaks with 2 lemons cut into wedges.

 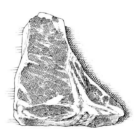

Figure 16.
The T-bone (right) combines an oblong piece of strip with
a round of tenderloin that measures less than 1¼ inch in diameter.
The grain of the strip piece is finer and more desirable than that of
the porterhouse because it's closer to the rib (not the hip). The
porterhouse (left) combines both strip and tenderloin, but the
tenderloin section is larger.

Figure 17.
Porterhouse and T-bone steaks contain portions of the delicate,
buttery tenderloin as well as some of the chewier, more
flavorful strip. When grilling these steaks, keep the tenderloin
(the smaller portion on the left side of the bone on these steaks)
over the cooler part of the fire.

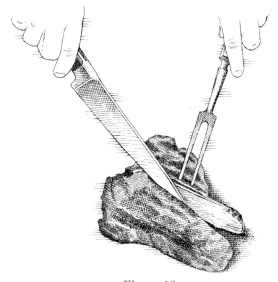

Figure 18.
Once grilled, let a porterhouse or T-bone steak rest for five minutes
before slicing and dividing the meat into two serving portions.
Start by slicing close to the bone to remove the strip section.

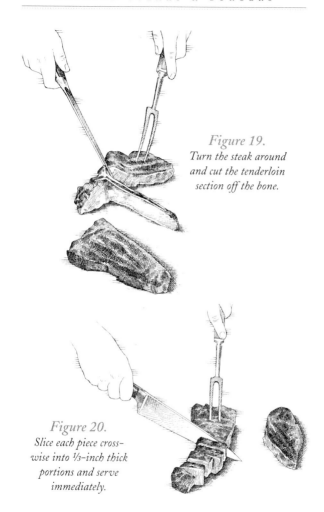

Figure 19.
Turn the steak around
and cut the tenderloin
section off the bone.

Figure 20.
Slice each piece cross-
wise into ⅓-inch thick
portions and serve
immediately.

Grilled London Broil

➤ **NOTE:** *London broil is a recipe, not a cut of meat. You take a thick steak, grill it, then slice it thinly, on a bias, across the grain. Traditionally, the cut for London broil was flank steak, which was once inexpensive but now costs upwards of $7 a pound. Thick steaks cut from the shoulder rather than the round (in our kitchen tests we found the latter to have a livery flavor and tougher texture) make a cheaper alternative, often selling for $2 or $3 a pound. This recipe can be adapted to thinner flanks. Simply grill over a single-level fire to desired doneness, 6 to 8 minutes total. Because the shoulder is thicker, it requires the two-level fire specified below. Do not cook past medium-rare or this lean cut will be unpalatably dry. London broil tastes best when served with a compound butter (see page 38). Serves four.*

1½–2   pounds boneless shoulder steak, about
          1½ inches thick
          Salt and ground black pepper

⠿ INSTRUCTIONS:

1. Build a two-level fire (*see* figure 4, page 16). Set grill rack in place, cover grill with lid, and let rack heat up, about 5 minutes.

2. Meanwhile, sprinkle both sides of steak with salt and pepper to taste. Grill, uncovered, until well browned on one side, 2 to 3 minutes. Turn steak; grill until well browned on second side, 2 to 3 minutes.

3. Once steak is well browned on both sides, slide to cooler part of grill. Continue grilling over medium fire to desired doneness, 5 to 6 minutes more for rare (120 degrees on instant-read thermometer), 6 to 7 minutes for medium-rare on the rare side (125 degrees), or 7 to 8 minutes for medium-rare on the medium side (130 degrees). Let steak rest 5 minutes, slice thin on bias, and serve immediately.

Figure 21.
A boneless shoulder steak about 1½ inches thick makes the tenderest,
most flavorful London broil when sliced thin on the bias.

Parsley Butter

➤ NOTE: *This recipe makes enough butter for four servings. If you like, double the recipe and freeze extra butter, wrapped tightly in plastic, for up to one month.*

2   tablespoons butter, softened
1   tablespoon minced fresh parsley leaves
1   tablespoon minced shallot, optional
    Salt and ground black pepper

⠿ INSTRUCTIONS:

Use fork to mash butter and parsley together in small bowl. Work in shallot if using and salt and pepper to taste. Wrap in plastic and shape into small log. Refrigerate until needed, slicing off pieces and letting melt over hot steaks.

⠿ VARIATIONS:

Parsley-Caper Butter

Add 1 teaspoon minced capers with parsley.

Lemon-Parsley Butter

Add 1 teaspoon grated lemon zest with parsley.

Roquefort Butter

Replace 1 tablespoon butter with ½ ounce crumbled Roquefort cheese. Omit parsley and shallot and add ¼ teaspoon brandy along with salt and pepper.

Grilled Burgers

➤ **N O T E :** *Chuck that you grind yourself or buy ground is the key to juicy, flavorful burgers. The meat should be 80 percent lean. Serves four, with buns and toppings.*

1¼	**pounds ground chuck**
¾	**teaspoon salt**
¼	**teaspoon ground black pepper**

▋ **I N S T R U C T I O N S :**

1. Build a single-level fire (*see* figure 3, page 15). Set grill rack in place, cover grill with lid, and let rack heat up, about 5 minutes.

2. Meanwhile, break up chuck to increase surface area for seasonings. Sprinkle salt and pepper over meat; toss lightly with hands to distribute seasonings. Divide meat into four equal portions and shape into burgers (*see* figures 22 and 23, pages 40 and 41).

3. Grill burgers, uncovered, over hot fire, turning once and cooking to desired doneness as follows: 3 minutes per side for rare, 4 minutes per side for medium-rare, 5 minutes on the first side and 4 minutes on second side for medium, and 5 minutes per side for well-done. Serve immediately.

Figure 22.
With cupped hands, toss one portion of meat back and forth from
hand to hand to shape into a loose ball.

40

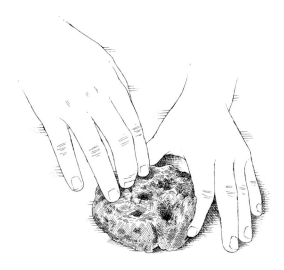

Figure 23.
Pat lightly to flatten into 1-inch-thick burger that measures 3½ to
4 inches across. Use fingertips to create pocked, textured surface.

chapter three

GRILLED PORK
TENDERLOIN
& CHOPS

T ODAY'S LEANER PORK DOES WELL ON THE grill as long as you are careful not to over-cook it. However, the tenderloin and chops can become tough and dry if cooked until thoroughly gray. This method worked for our mothers when even "lean" cuts of pork were laced with fat. But today we recommend grilling both the tenderloin and chops until the center is just tinged with a little pink (not bloody) in the center. The meat will register about 150 degrees on an instant-read thermometer at this stage.

The tenderloin is a torpedo-shaped cut that runs along the rib bones in the loin section. It is extremely lean and notable for its lack of marbling. While tender, it can be bland and benefits greatly from assertive seasoning. We prefer to coat the tenderloin (as well as chops) with a spice or herb rub before grilling and then serve it with a salsa, which adds more flavor and moisture. While a little sweetness often accentuates the flavor of pork, a sweet rub can burn easily, so tend the grill carefully when adding sugar to the mix.

Pork chops were once much fattier and less prone to drying out. While the problem is not quite as acute as with the tenderloin, care must be taken when cooking chops to keep them moist. When buying pork chops, look for chops that are solidly pink rather than streaked with white—the white is not fat but connective tissue, mostly elastin, which does not break down during cooking. Also, be sure to buy chops that are an inch thick. Thinner chops will dry out by the time the exterior is nicely seared.

The two "center-cut" chops (*see* figure 25, page 47) are taken from the center of the loin and are our first choice for grilling. The center rib chop looks like a miniature beef rib and the center loin chop looks like a miniature T-bone or porterhouse steak. Avoid cuts from the end of the loin, which tend to be tough and sinewy. Like the tenderloin, chops can be a bit dry and bland when simply oiled and seasoned with salt and pepper. Serve them with salsa and rub with spices or herbs for extra flavor and moisture.

Grilled Pork Tenderloin

➤ **NOTE:** *Tenderloins come two to a package, each weighing a little less than a pound and serving four to six depending on the side dishes. Invariably one tenderloin is smaller than the other and will require 2 or 3 minutes less time on the grill. We like pork cooked medium, just until a tinge of pink remains in the center. You may cook pork until well done (about 160 degrees), but it will be a bit drier. Season with salt and pepper as directed below or coat with a spice or herb rub (see page 48). Either way, serve with a salsa (see page 49).*

2	pork tenderloins (about 2 pounds total), silver skin trimmed (*see* figure 24)
2	tablespoons extra-virgin olive oil
	Salt and ground black pepper

⸬ **INSTRUCTIONS:**

1. Build a single-level fire (*see* figure 3, page 15). Set grill rack in place, cover grill with lid, and let rack heat up, about 5 minutes.

2. Rub tenderloins with oil and sprinkle with salt and pepper to taste. Grill over medium-hot fire, turning several times to make sure all four sides are browned, about 4 minutes per side. Cover tenderloins with disposable aluminum roasting pan (*see* figure 29, page 63). Cook, turning once, until meat is tinged with pink in center or internal temperature registers

150 degrees, 5 to 7 minutes. Let tenderloins rest for 5 minutes, slice crosswise into 1-inch-thick pieces, and serve immediately with salsa or other sauce.

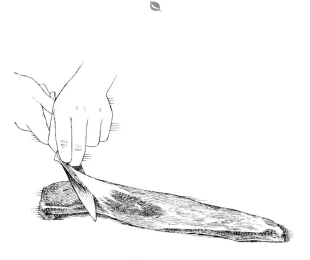

Figure 24.
To remove the silver skin, slip a paring knife between the silver skin and the muscle fibers. Angle the knife slightly upward and use a gentle back-and-forth sawing action.

Grilled Pork Chops

➤ NOTE: *We prefer center loin or center rib chops (*see *figure 25, page 47) that are an inch thick for grilling. They can be seasoned with just salt and pepper, but we prefer them when coated with a spice or herb rub (*see *page 48) and served with salsa (*see *page 49). Serves four.*

    4   center loin or center rib pork chops, each
         1-inch thick (about 2 pounds total)
    2   tablespoons extra-virgin olive oil
         Salt and ground black pepper

⁞ INSTRUCTIONS:

1. Build a two-level fire (*see* figure 4, page 16). Set grill rack in place, cover grill with lid, and let rack heat up, about 5 minutes.

2. Rub chops with oil and sprinkle with salt and pepper to taste. Grill over medium-hot fire, turning once, until both sides are browned, about 6 minutes.

3. Slide chops to cooler part of fire and cover with disposable aluminum roasting pan (*see* figure 29, page 63). Grill over medium-low fire, turning once, until meat is tinged with pink in center, 8 to 10 minutes. Serve immediately.

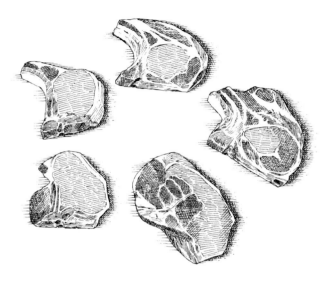

Figure 25.
There are five kinds of pork chops regularly available in supermarkets and butcher shops. Clockwise from the top, the rib end,
the rib end blade, the sirloin end, the center loin, and the center
rib. We prefer the center loin and center rib chops, which are
meatier and less chewy than the rest.

47

Spice Rub for Pork

➤ NOTE: *Because this rub contains sugar, make sure to mind the grill and turn the pork often to keep the sugar from burning.*

1	tablespoon fennel seeds
1	tablespoon cumin seeds
1	tablespoon coriander seeds
¾	teaspoon ground cinnamon
1½	teaspoons dry mustard
1½	teaspoons brown sugar

INSTRUCTIONS:

Toast seeds in small skillet over medium heat, shaking pan occasionally to prevent burning, until first wisps of smoke appear, 3 to 5 minutes. Cool to room temperature, mix with remaining ingredients, and grind to powder in spice grinder. Rub mixture over oiled and seasoned pork before grilling.

VARIATION:

Herb Rub for Pork

Grind following ingredients in spice grinder: 1½ teaspoons each dried thyme, dried rosemary, and black peppercorns; 2 bay leaves, crumbled; 2 whole cloves or allspice berries; and 1 teaspoon salt. Do not sprinkle pork with salt or pepper.

Pineapple Salsa

➤ NOTE: *This sweet salsa complements grilled pork nicely. The moisture also keeps the pork from tasting dry.*

¼	small pineapple, peeled, cored, and dice d
1	barely ripe banana, peeled and diced
½	cup seedless green grapes, halved or quartered
½	firm avocado, peeled and cut into ⅜-inch dice
4	teaspoons lime juice
1	jalapeño chile, stemmed, seeded, and minced
1	teaspoon minced fresh oregano leaves
	Salt

INSTRUCTIONS:

Combine all ingredients including salt to taste in medium bowl. Let stand at room temperature for 30 minutes. Serve alongside grilled pork tenderloin or chops.

VARIATION:

Peach Salsa

Combine following ingredients and refrigerate for at least 1 hour or up to 4 days: 2 chopped peaches, 1 diced red bell pepper, 1 small diced red onion, ¼ cup chopped parsley, 1 minced garlic clove, ¼ cup pineapple juice, 6 tablespoons lime juice, 1 minced jalapeño, and salt to taste.

chapter four

ᘓ

GRILLED LAMB CHOPS

GRILLED LAMB CHOPS DON'T HAVE TO BE A rare (and expensive) summer treat. True, loin and rib chops (together, the eight rib chops form the cut known as rack of lamb) can cost upwards of $12 a pound. But we love the meaty flavor and chewy (but not tough) texture of shoulder chops. We also like the fact that they cost just $4 per pound.

In a side-by-side taste test, we grilled loin, rib, and shoulder chops to medium-rare and let them stand about 5 minutes before tasting. The rib chop was the most refined of the three, with a mild, almost sweet flavor and tender texture. The loin chop had a slightly stronger flavor; the texture was a bit firmer (but not chewier) than the rib chop. The shoulder chop had a distinctly gutsier flavor than the other two. While it was not at all tough, it was chewier. If you like the flavor of lamb (and we do) and are trying to keep within a budget, then try shoulder chops.

We also tried a second test in which we grilled the chops to medium, a stage at which many people prefer lamb. Both the rib and loin chops were dry and less flavorful and juicy than they were at medium-rare. The shoulder chop held its own, in both taste and texture, displaying another advantage besides price.

Shoulder chops can range in thickness from ½ to 1 inch. We prefer the thicker chops and you should ask your butcher to cut them for you if necessary. Loin and rib chops are usually thicker, often close to 1½ inches. The added thickness means that these chops should be cooked over a two-level fire to bring the inside up to temperature without charring the exterior. A two-level fire also makes sense as lamb tends to flame and the cooler part of the grill is the perfect place to let flames die down. Even when making a single-level fire for thinner shoulder chops, we often leave part of the grill bottom uncovered with coals so that we have a place to slide the chops if the flames become too intense.

Grilled Shoulder Lamb Chops

➤ **NOTE:** *Grill shoulder lamb chops over a very hot fire. Half-inch-thick chops, which many supermarkets sell, require about 30 seconds less cooking time per side. Serves four.*

> 4   **shoulder lamb chops (blade or round bone),**
>   **about ¾ inch thick**
> 2   **tablespoons extra-virgin olive oil**
>   **Salt and ground black pepper**

⬛ INSTRUCTIONS:

1. Build a single-level fire (*see* figure 3, page 15). Set grill rack in place, cover grill with lid, and let rack heat up, about 5 minutes.

2. Rub chops with oil and sprinkle with salt and pepper to taste. Grill over hot fire until bottom of each chop is well browned, about 2 minutes. (If chops start to flame, pull off heat for a moment or extinguish flames with squirt bottle.) Turn each chop and cook about 2 minutes more for medium-rare or 2½ minutes for medium. Serve immediately.

⬛ VARIATIONS:

Grilled Lamb Chops with Garlic-Rosemary Marinade

Stir 2 large garlic cloves, put through a press or pureed, 1 tablespoon minced fresh rosemary leaves, and pinch cayenne into oil. Rub chops with paste; let stand at least 30 minutes. (Chops can be refrigerated overnight.) Grill as directed.

52

Grilled Lamb Chops with Soy-Shallot Marinade

Stir ¼ cup minced shallot or scallion, 2 tablespoons each minced fresh thyme and parsley leaves, 3 tablespoons lemon juice, and 2 tablespoons soy sauce into oil. Marinate chops in mixture for at least 20 minutes, or up to 1 hour. Grill as directed.

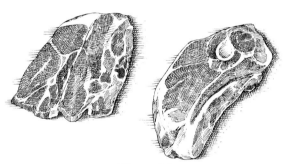

Figure 26.
There are two kinds of shoulder chops. The blade chop (left) is roughly rectangular in shape and contains a piece of the chine bone and a thin piece of the blade bone. The arm or round bone chop (right) is leaner and contains a round cross-section of the arm bone so that the chop looks a bit like a mini ham steak. The extra fat in the blade chop melts on the grill, flavoring and moistening the meat. The arm bone chop has a tiny line of riblets on the side of each chop, which are delicious. Either chop takes well to grilling.

Grilled Loin or Rib Lamb Chops

➤ **N O T E :** *Because loin and rib chops are thicker than shoulder chops, they must first be seared over a hot fire and then cooked through on a cooler part of the grill. These chops are smaller than shoulder chops and you will need two for each serving. Use either of the marinades on pages 52 and 53 with these chops.*

    8   **loin or frenched rib lamb chops, each about 1¼ inches thick**

    2   **tablespoons extra-virgin olive oil**
           Salt and ground black pepper

I N S T R U C T I O N S :

1. Build a two-level fire (*see* figure 4, page 16). Set grill rack in place, cover grill with lid, and let rack heat up, about 5 minutes.

2. Rub chops with oil and sprinkle with salt and pepper to taste. Grill over hot fire, turning once, for 4 minutes. (If chops start to flame, pull off heat for a moment or extinguish flames with squirt bottle.) Move chops to cooler part of grill and continue grilling over medium fire, turning once, until desired doneness, about 6 minutes for rare and 8 minutes for medium. Serve immediately.

5 4

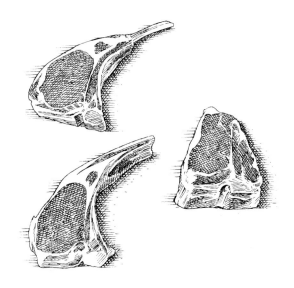

Figure 27.
Rib chops (bottom left) often contain a lot of fat on the bone.
Have your butcher "french" the chop (top left) by scraping away
this fat. Like a T-bone steak, a loin chop (right) has meat on
either side of the bone. The small piece on the right side of the
bone is very tender and fine-grained. The larger piece on the
left side is chewier.

chapter five

GRILLED
CHICKEN

A S SOON AS OUR TESTING STARTED, WE REAL-
ized we needed to develop separate methods
for dark and white meat parts. The higher
fat content in thighs and legs makes flare-
ups a greater problem, while the breasts have a tendency to
dry out and need special handling.

We quickly dismissed partially cooking before or after
grilling, since poaching or microwaving yielded dry, cottony
meat. Finishing grilled parts in a hot oven is cumbersome
and the grill flavor is not strong enough.

We tried the method recommended by the manufacturers of many covered grills: searing chicken over a hot fire,

then moving it to a medium fire, putting the cover on, and cooking until done. This method works well, but the residue on the inside of the cover imparts an undesirable flavor.

Next, we tried searing the chicken over a medium-hot fire and then moving it to a medium fire to finish cooking. This approach was fine for thinner thighs and legs. However, we found that breasts need to be moved to an area with no coals and covered with a disposable pan (no off flavors here) to cook through.

Marinating the chicken does not add much flavor and causes constant flare-ups during the initial searing period. Rubbing the chicken with a spice rub prior to grilling proved far more satisfactory. Barbecue sauces often contain some sweetener and can burn if brushed on the chicken before cooking. We found it best to brush them on when cooking was almost done As a final test, we tried brining the chicken before grilling it. The brine penetrated the chicken, seasoning it and slightly firming up its texture before grilling.

You can grill dark and white meat parts together, if you like. Set up a three-level fire with most of the coals on one side of the grill, some coals in the middle, and no coals on the opposite side. Sear all the chicken parts over the hottest part of the fire, finish cooking the legs and thighs over the medium fire in the middle, and move the seared breasts to the coolest part of the grill and cover with a disposable pan.

Grilled Chicken Thighs or Legs

➤ NOTE: *Brining improves the chicken's flavor, but if you're short on time, skip step 1 and season the chicken generously with salt and pepper before cooking. Add flavorings or during cooking: Rub the chicken parts with a spice rub or paste (see pages 64 and 65) before they go on the grill or brush them with barbecue sauce (see page 66) during the final 2 minutes of cooking. Serves four.*

8	chicken thighs or 4 whole legs
¾	cup kosher salt or 6 tablespoons table salt
¾	cup sugar
	Ground black pepper

∷ INSTRUCTIONS:

1. Trim overhanging fat and skin from chicken pieces; this will prevent burning. In gallon-size zipper-lock plastic bag, dissolve salt and sugar in 1 quart of water. Add chicken, seal bag, and refrigerate until fully seasoned, about 1½ hours.

2. Build a two-level fire (*see* figure 4, page 16). Set grill rack in place, cover grill with lid, and let rack heat up, about 5 minutes.

3. Meanwhile, remove chicken from brine, rinse well, dry thoroughly with paper towels, and season with pepper to taste or one of the spice rubs or pastes on pages 64–67.

4. Cook chicken, uncovered, over medium-hot fire until seared, about 1 to 2 minutes on each side. Move chicken to medium fire; continue to grill uncovered, turning occasionally, until dark and fully cooked, 12 to 16 minutes for thighs, 16 to 20 minutes for whole legs. To test for doneness, either peek into thickest part of chicken with tip of small knife (you should see no redness near the bone) or check internal temperature at thickest part with instant-read thermometer, which should register 165 degrees. Transfer to serving platter. Serve warm or at room temperature.

Grilled Bone-In Chicken Breasts

➤ NOTE: *If the fire flares because of dripping fat or a gust of wind, move the chicken to the area without coals until the flames die down. See note on page 58 about flavoring chicken and omitting the brining step when pressed for time. Serves four.*

¾	cup kosher salt or 6 tablespoons table salt
¾	cup sugar
4	split chicken breasts (bone-in, skin-on), 10 to 12 ounces each
	Ground black pepper

▓ INSTRUCTIONS:

1. In gallon-size zipper-lock plastic bag, dissolve salt and sugar in 1 quart of water. Add chicken, seal bag, and refrigerate until fully seasoned, about 1½ hours.

2. Build a two-level fire but do not spread coals out over half of grill (*see* figure 28, page 62). Set grill rack in place, cover grill with lid, and let rack heat up, about 5 minutes.

3. Meanwhile, remove chicken from brine, rinse well, dry thoroughly with paper towels, and season with pepper to taste or one of the spice rubs or pastes on pages 64 and 65.

4. Cook chicken, uncovered, over medium-hot fire until well browned, 2 to 3 minutes per side. Move chicken to area with no fire and cover with disposable aluminum roasting pan; continue to cook, skin side up, 10 minutes (*see* figure 29, page 63). Turn and cook 5 minutes more. To test for doneness, either peek into thickest part of chicken with tip of small knife (you should see no redness near the bone) or check internal temperature at thickest part with instant-read thermometer, which should register 160 degrees. Transfer to serving platter. Serve warm or at room temperature.

Figure 28.
Thick bone–in chicken breasts are so susceptible to burning on the
grill that we build an unusual two-level fire with all the coals
piled high on half the grill (for searing) and the remaining part
of the grill empty (for cooking through).

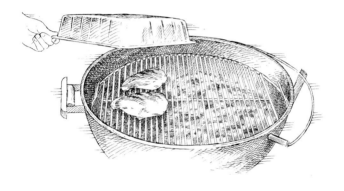

Figure 29.

To trap heat and speed up the cooking process over the cool part
of the fire, cover the chicken breasts with a disposable roasting
pan. The pan creates an oven-like effect and protects the skin
from further coloring. We also use this technique with pork
tenderloin and chops.

Basic Spice Rub for Chicken

➤ NOTE: *Use this rub (or the variation) prior to grilling. Makes about ½ cup, enough to coat a single recipe of either dark or white meat parts.*

2	tablespoons ground cumin
2	tablespoons curry powder
2	tablespoons chili powder
1	tablespoon ground allspice
1	tablespoon ground black pepper
1	teaspoon ground cinnamon

INSTRUCTIONS:

Combine all ingredients in small bowl. Rub mixture over brined and dried chicken parts before grilling.

VARIATION:

Garam Masala Spice Rub

Toast following ingredients in dry skillet until fragrant, about 2 minutes, and then grind to powder in spice grinder: 2 tablespoons each fennel seeds, anise seeds, cardamom pods, and black peppercorns; 1 teaspoon whole cloves; and 1 cinnamon stick, broken into several pieces.

Basic Spice Paste for Chicken with Citrus and Cilantro

➤ **NOTE:** *Makes about ⅓ cup, enough to season a single recipe of either dark or white meat parts.*

1	teaspoon ground cumin
1	teaspoon chili powder
1	teaspoon paprika
1	teaspoon ground coriander
2	tablespoons orange juice
1	tablespoon lime juice
1	tablespoon olive oil
1	garlic clove, peeled
2	tablespoons fresh cilantro leaves

INSTRUCTIONS:

Puree all ingredients in food processor or blender until smooth. Rub paste over brined and dried chicken parts before grilling.

VARIATION:

Asian Spice Paste

Replace spices, juices, and olive oil with 1 tablespoon minced fresh chile, 1 tablespoon chopped fresh gingerroot, 2 tablespoons soy sauce, and 2 tablespoons peanut oil.

Basic Barbecue Sauce

➤ **NOTE:** *This recipe makes about 3 cups, enough for several batches of chicken.*

2	tablespoons vegetable oil
1	medium onion, minced
1	can (8 ounces) tomato sauce
1	can (28 ounces) whole tomatoes with juice
¾	cup distilled white vinegar
¼	cup packed dark brown sugar
2	tablespoons molasses
1	tablespoon paprika
1	tablespoon chili powder
2	teaspoons liquid smoke, optional
1	teaspoon salt
2	teaspoons ground black pepper
¼	cup orange juice

⊞ INSTRUCTIONS:

1. Heat oil in large, heavy-bottomed saucepan over medium heat. Add onion and sauté, stirring frequently, until golden brown, 7 to 10 minutes. Add remaining ingredients. Bring to boil, reduce heat to lowest possible setting, and simmer, uncovered, until thickened, 2 to 2½ hours.

2. Puree sauce, in batches if necessary, in food processor or blender. Transfer to airtight container. (Can be refrigerated for 2 weeks.)

3. Brush chicken parts with sauce about 2 minutes before they are done, turning and brushing again after 1 minute.

▪▪ VARIATIONS:

Barbecue Sauce with Mexican Flavors

To completed and cooled sauce, add 1½ teaspoons ground cumin, 1½ teaspoons chili powder, 6 tablespoons lime juice, and 3 tablespoons chopped fresh cilantro leaves.

Barbecue Sauce with Asian Flavors

To completed and cooled sauce, add 1 tablespoon minced fresh gingerroot, 6 tablespoons soy sauce, 6 tablespoons rice wine vinegar, 3 tablespoons sugar, and 1½ tablespoons Asian sesame oil.

chapter six

GRILLED SEAFOOD

S ALMON IS THE EASIEST FISH TO GRILL BECAUSE it is oily, and therefore harder to overcook. However, salmon often sticks to the grill and tears. Our testing revealed that a medium-hot fire browns without burning and, more importantly, creates the necessary crust so that the salmon can be flipped easily. Oiling the skin does not keep it from sticking and can cause flare-ups. We prefer to rub the grill grate with a wad of paper towels dipped in vegetable oil before cooking any fish.

Center-cut fillets are almost always 1½ inches thick and ideal for grilling; thinner pieces cut from the tail tend to

68

overcook, and thick pieces from the head can take too long to cook through. The grill cover can impart a smoky, fatty flavor to the fish, so leave it off.

Tuna and swordfish have much less fat than salmon, so drying out is a real threat on the grill. By the time these steaks are seared, the inside can be dry and unappetizingly fishy, especially if the steaks are thin. We found a hot fire will produce well-seared fish that is moist inside.

If you want these fish rare or medium-rare, they must be cut about 1½ inches thick. But you can't always get thick steaks. The standard supermarket cut is ¾ to 1 inch thick. By the time a piece of tuna or swordfish this thin is seared, the fish is overcooked. Something must be done to thin-cut tuna and swordfish before it hits the grill. After testing various marinades, we found that soaking the fish in olive oil does the best job of keeping the texture moist and luscious, even in thin steaks cooked to medium and beyond.

According to the food scientists we spoke with, the oil penetrates and coats the strands of protein in tuna and swordfish so that the fish feels moist in the mouth, even after most of the moisture has been cooked out. Oils high in emulsifiers—such as mono- and di-glycerides—penetrate protein more quickly than oils containing less of these agents. Extra-virgin olive oil contains both these emulsifiers and also adds flavor to the fish.

Grilled Salmon

➤ **NOTE:** *If your fillets are less than 1½ inches thick, decrease the grilling time by roughly 30 seconds per side. To test fillets for doneness, either peek into the salmon with the tip of a small knife, or remove the salmon from the grill and squeeze both sides of the fillet gently with your fingertips (raw salmon is squishy; medium-rare salmon is firm, but not hard). Serves four.*

> Vegetable oil for grill grate
> 4   center-cut salmon fillets, each 6 to 7 ounces and 1½ inches thick, pin bones removed (*see* figures 30 and 31, page 72)
> Salt and ground black pepper

⠿ INSTRUCTIONS:

1. Build a single-level fire (*see* figure 3, page 15). Set grill rack in place, cover grill with lid, and let rack heat up, about 5 minutes. Rub cooking grate with oil-dipped wad of paper towels (see figure 32, page 73).

2. Generously sprinkle each side of fillets with salt and pepper. Place fillets skin side down on grill. Grill over medium-hot fire until skin shrinks and separates from flesh and turns black, 2 to 3 minutes. Flip fillets gently with long-handled tongs or spatula. Grill until fillets are opaque throughout, yet translucent at very center, 3 to 4 minutes. Serve immediately.

Grilled Salmon with Mustard Glaze

Mix 2 tablespoons each dry mustard and sugar with 2 tea-spoons water to make thick paste. Sprinkle fish with salt and pepper and spread paste over flesh side of fillets. Grill as directed, drizzling with extra-virgin olive oil before serving.

Grilled Salmon with Indian Flavors and Mango Chutney

For marinade, mix 2 tablespoons vegetable oil, 2 table-spoons grated fresh gingerroot, 1½ teaspoons each ground cumin, coriander, and salt, and ¼ teaspoon cayenne pepper in shallow bowl. Marinate salmon while coals are heating and do not sprinkle with salt and pepper. For chutney, mix 1 ripe mango cut into ½-inch dice, 3 tablespoons lemon juice, and 1 tablespoon chopped fresh cilantro leaves in small bowl. Grill as directed and serve with chutney.

Figure 30.
Using the tips of your fingers, gently rub the surface of each
salmon fillet to locate any pin bones.

Figure 31.
If you find any bones, use a pair of needle-nose pliers to pull
them out.

Figure 32.
Just before placing fish on the grill, dip a large wad of paper towels in vegetable oil, grab it with tongs, and wipe the grid thoroughly to lubricate and prevent sticking. This will also clean any remaining residue from the grill.

73

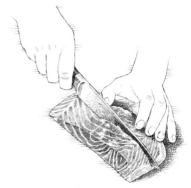

Figure 33.
Because they are thinner at the edges, salmon fillets do not cook through evenly. We like the gradation from well-done at the edges to rare in the center, but not everyone does. Steaks, which have an even thickness throughout, cook more evenly, but are bony. However, it is possible to turn a fillet into a steak. Start by cutting through a 3-inch-wide fillet lengthwise down to, but not through, the skin.

Figure 34.
Fold the two flesh pieces out with the skin acting as a hinge.

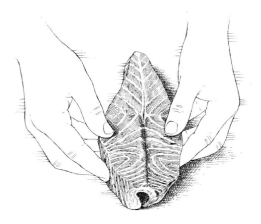

Figure 35.

A 3-inch-wide fillet will now look like a steak, but without any bones, and have an even thickness of 1½ inches. The one drawback is that the skin won't crisp since it is sandwiched in the middle of the steak. If you like to eat the skin, cook the fillets as is. The cooking time for mock steaks is the same as for regular fillets.

Thick-Cut Grilled Tuna

➤ **NOTE:** *If you like your tuna rare, you must buy steaks cut about 1½ inches thick. This will allow you to sear them well without overcooking the inside. For four, you'll need two steaks (they run about 1 pound each). Cut each in half before grilling. If you prefer more well-done tuna, buy thinner steaks and marinate in olive oil to keep them moist.*

> 2   **tuna steaks, cut 1½ inches thick**
>   **(about 1 pound each)**
> 2   **tablespoons extra-virgin olive oil**
>   **Salt and ground black pepper**

▦ **INSTRUCTIONS:**

1. Build a single-level fire (*see* figure 3, page 15). Set grill rack in place, cover grill with lid, and let rack heat up, about 5 minutes. Rub cooking grate with oil-dipped wad of paper towels (*see* figure 32, page 73).

2. Cut tuna steaks in half to make four equal pieces. Brush with oil and sprinkle with salt and pepper to taste.

3. Grill, turning once, over hot fire to desired doneness, about 5 to 6 minutes for rare or 7 to 8 minutes for medium-rare.

Thin-Cut Grilled Tuna

Combine 4 tuna steaks cut ¾- to 1-inch thick with ¼ cup extra-virgin olive oil in plastic zipper-lock bag. Marinate in refrigerator, turning several times, for at least 2 hours or overnight. Remove fish from bag, sprinkle with salt and pepper, and grill over hot fire to desired doneness, about 2½ minutes total for medium-rare, 3 minutes total for medium, and 4 minutes total for well-done.

Grilled Tuna with Herb-Infused Oil

Heat ¼ cup extra-virgin olive oil, 1½ teaspoons grated lemon zest, 1½ teaspoons chopped fresh thyme leaves, 1 minced garlic clove, and ¼ teaspoon hot red pepper flakes in small saucepan until hot. Cool oil and then brush some on thick-cut tuna before and after grilling. Use herb oil as marinade for thin-cut tuna.

Thick-Cut Grilled Swordfish

➤ **N O T E :** *Unlike salmon and tuna, we find that swordfish should be cooked until medium—no more or less. A two-level fire is necessary; the fish sears over the hot fire and then cooks through on the cooler part of the grill. If you can only find thin steaks, see variation below. Individual swordfish steaks are quite large. This recipe serves four, or more if you are willing to cut the steaks into smaller pieces.*

2	swordfish steaks, cut 1½ inches thick (about 1¼ pounds each)
2	tablespoons extra-virgin olive oil
	Salt and ground black pepper
	Lemon wedges

▦ **I N S T R U C T I O N S :**

1. Build a two-level fire (*see* figure 4, page 16). Set grill rack in place, cover grill with lid, and let rack heat up, about 5 minutes. Rub cooking grate with oil-dipped wad of paper towels (*see* figure 32, page 73).

2. Cut swordfish steaks in half to make four equal pieces. Brush with oil and sprinkle with salt and pepper to taste.

3. Grill, turning once, over hot fire for 9 minutes. Move fish to cooler part of grill and cook over medium fire, turning once, until center is no longer translucent, 4 to 6 minutes. Serve immediately with lemon wedges.

Thin-Cut Grilled Swordfish Steaks

Combine 4 swordfish steaks cut ¾- to 1-inch thick with ¼ cup extra-virgin olive oil in plastic zipper-lock bag. Marinate in refrigerator, turning several times, for at least 2 hours or overnight. Remove fish from bag and sprinkle with salt and pepper. Build single-level fire and grill over hot fire, turning once, until center is no longer translucent, about 6 minutes total.

Grilled Swordfish with Lemon-Parsley Sauce

Add 1 teaspoon grated lemon zest to olive oil for brushing on thicker steaks or marinating thinner cuts. Combine another ¼ cup extra-virgin olive oil with 1½ tablespoons lemon juice, 2 tablespoons minced fresh parsley leaves, and salt and pepper to taste in small bowl. Grill fish and serve with lemon-parsley sauce.

Grilled Swordfish with Salsa Verde

Combine 2 tablespoons minced fresh parsley leaves, 1 tablespoon minced fresh basil leaves, 1 tablespoon pitted and minced green olives, 1½ teaspoons drained and minced capers, 1 medium minced garlic clove, 1 minced flat anchovy fillet, 2 tablespoons extra-virgin olive oil, 1 tablespoon lemon juice, and pepper to taste in small bowl. Grill fish and serve with sauce.

Grilled Shrimp with Garlic Paste

➤ N O T E : *Brining dramatically improves the taste and texture of shrimp. To keep shrimp moist, grill them with the shell on. Thread on skewers or grill over mesh screen to keep them from falling onto the coals.*

1	cup plus 1 teaspoon kosher salt
2	pounds medium shrimp in the shell
2	large garlic cloves, peeled
1	teaspoon cayenne pepper
2	teaspoons paprika
¼	cup extra-virgin olive oil
4	teaspoons lemon juice
	Lemon wedges

▓ I N S T R U C T I O N S :

1. Dissolve 1 cup salt in 1 quart warm water in large bowl. Add another quart of cold water along with shrimp, and let stand for 45 minutes. Drain and rinse thoroughly under cold running water.

2. Build a single-level fire (*see* figure 3, page 15). Set grill rack in place, cover grill with lid, and let rack heat up, about 5 minutes.

3. Meanwhile, mince garlic with remaining 1 teaspoon salt to form smooth paste. Mix with cayenne and paprika in small bowl. Stir in oil and lemon juice. Toss shrimp with paste until evenly coated. Thread shrimp on skewers (*see* figures 36–38, pages 82 and 83) if desired.

4. Grill shrimp over medium fire, turning once, until shells turn bright pink, 2 to 3 minutes per side. Serve hot or at room temperature with lemon wedges.

▒ **VARIATION:**

Grilled Shrimp with Anchovy Butter

Omit garlic paste. Pour contents of 2-ounce can of flat anchovy fillets packed in olive oil into small saucepan. Turn heat to medium-low and cook, mashing anchovies with wooden spoon, until fillets fall apart and form smooth sauce, about 3 minutes. Add 4 tablespoons unsalted butter and 1½ teaspoons lemon juice. Cook just until butter melts; keep sauce warm. Toss shrimp with 1 tablespoon olive oil, grill, and then toss with anchovy butter and serve with lemon wedges.

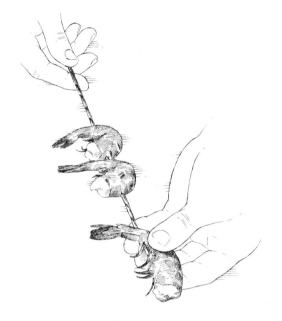

Figure 36.
Shrimp may be threaded by passing a single skewer through the
body near the tail, folding the shrimp over, and passing the
skewer through the body again near the head.

82

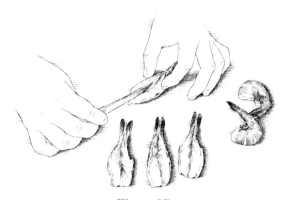

Figure 37.
Shrimp can also be butterflied and threaded on two skewers.
Use a sharp paring knife to slice through the back and cut about
two-thirds of the way through the shrimp.

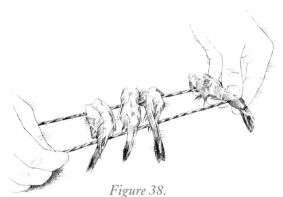

Figure 38.
Push one skewer through both sides of the butterflied shrimp near
the head. Push a second skewer through the shrimp near the tail.

83

chapter seven

GRILLED
VEGETABLES

EGETABLES DON'T RESPOND WELL TO BLAZING fires—incineration is a real possibility. A medium-hot fire (you should be able to hold your hand five inches off the grate for four seconds) is ideal for most vegetables. A few, slower-cooking items, such as new potatoes, or particularly delicate vegetables, such as asparagus, are better cooked over a medium or medium-low fire.

Because even a cheap gas grill has enough BTUs to reach these heat levels, the type of grill used to cook vegetables is not very important. Delicate vegetables can pick up some resinous flavor from the cover, so leave it off. It is also imperative that the grate be scraped clean. Tiny bits of charred-on food cause flare-ups (which must be avoided at all costs when grilling veggies) and can impart an off flavor.

We tested various grill equipment designed for vegetables and found it best to cook vegetables right on the grate. (Hinged metal baskets are not practical because some vegetables will cook faster than others, and in these baskets everything must be turned at the same time.) Smaller items like cherry tomatoes or mushrooms can be skewered to keep them from falling through the grill grate. A vegetable grid (a tightly woven grid with handles) or piece of fine mesh can be set right on the cooking grate to keep small items and onions from falling onto the coals.

The following vegetables work best on the grill, all without any precooking. Toss or brush each vegetable with extra-virgin olive oil (other oils are too bland) before grilling and cook over a medium-hot fire unless otherwise specified. If you like, add salt and pepper, fresh herbs, garlic, and/or grated citrus zest to the oil before brushing it on vegetables, or try one of the flavored oils sold at supermarkets. Grilled vegetables can also be seasoned with salt and pepper just before serving.

■■ ASPARAGUS: Snap off tough ends. Grill over medium fire, turning several times, until tender and streaked with light grill marks, 6 to 8 minutes.

⠿ CORN: Remove husk and silk. Grill over medium fire, turning often, until kernels start to char, about 4 minutes.

⠿ EGGPLANT: Remove ends. Cut large eggplant cross-wise into ½-inch-thick rounds. Slice small eggplant length-wise into ½-inch-thick strips; if you like, remove the peel from outer slices so they match other pieces (*see* figure 40, page 90). Grill, turning once, until flesh is darkly colored, 8 to 10 minutes.

⠿ ENDIVE: Cut in half lengthwise through stem end. Grill, flat side down, until streaked with dark grill marks, 6 to 8 minutes.

⠿ FENNEL: Remove stalks and fronds. Slice vertically through base into ½-inch-thick pieces. Grill, turning once, until streaked with dark grill marks and quite soft, 10 to 15 minutes.

⠿ MUSHROOMS, PORTOBELLO: Clean with damp cloth and remove stems. Grill, with gill-like underside facing up, until cap is streaked with grill marks, 8 to 10 minutes.

⠿ MUSHROOMS, WHITE BUTTON AND CREMINI: Clean with damp cloth and trim thin slice from stems. Grill on grid, turning several times, until golden brown, 6 to 7 minutes.

⠿ ONIONS: Peel and cut into ½-inch-thick slices. Grill on grid, turning once, until lightly charred, about 6 minutes.

▪▪ PEPPERS: Core, seed, and cut into large wedges. Grill, turning once, until streaked with dark grill marks, 9 to 10 minutes.

▪▪ POTATOES, NEW: Choose very small potatoes (no larger than whole walnut) and cut them in half. Grill on grid over medium-low fire, turning several times, until richly colored and tender throughout, 25 to 30 minutes.

▪▪ TOMATOES, CHERRY: Remove stems. Grill on grid, turning several times, until streaked with dark grill marks, about 3 minutes.

▪▪ TOMATOES, PLUM: Cut in half lengthwise and seed. Grill, turning once, until streaked with dark grill marks, about 8 minutes.

▪▪ ZUCCHINI (AND SUMMER SQUASH): Remove ends. Slice lengthwise into ½-inch-thick strips. If you like, remove the peel from outer slices so they match other pieces (*see* figure 40, page 90). Grill, turning once, until streaked with dark grill marks, 8 to 10 minutes.

Grilled Italian Vegetables with Thyme and Garlic

➢ NOTE: *A vegetable grid (see figure 39, page 90) is essential for grilling onions. Drizzle vegetables with balsamic vinegar at the table if you like. Serves six.*

½	cup extra-virgin olive oil
3	medium garlic cloves, minced
1	tablespoon minced fresh thyme leaves, plus several sprigs for garnish
	Salt and ground black pepper
3	medium zucchini (about 1 pound), ends trimmed and cut lengthwise into ½-inch-thick strips
3	small eggplant (about 1 pound), ends trimmed and cut lengthwise into ½-inch-thick strips
2	large red onions (about 1 pound), peeled and cut into ½-inch-thick slices
1	large red bell pepper, cored, seeded, and cut into large wedges

■■ INSTRUCTIONS:

1. Build a single-level fire (*see* figure 3, page 15). Set grill rack in place, cover grill with lid, and let rack heat up, about 5 minutes.

2. Meanwhile, combine oil, garlic, minced thyme, and salt and pepper to taste in small bowl. Lay vegetables on large baking sheet or platter and brush with flavored oil.

3. Place vegetable grid over medium-hot fire and heat for several minutes. Spread onions out over grid in single layer. Place remaining vegetables on open parts of grill. If necessary, vegetables can be grilled in batches.

4. Grill over medium-hot fire, turning vegetables once, until everything is marked with dark stripes, about 6 minutes for onions and 8 to 10 minutes for zucchini, eggplant, and pepper.

5. As each vegetable looks done, transfer it to large platter. Garnish platter with thyme sprigs and serve grilled vegetables hot, warm, or at room temperature. (Vegetables can be covered and kept at room temperature for several hours.)

Figure 39.

A vegetable grid has tightly woven bars of metal that keep small items such as onions from falling through the cooking grate. Set the vegetable grid directly onto the grate and then cook onions, small mushrooms, or cherry tomatoes on the grid.

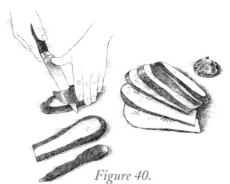

Figure 40.

For aesthetic reasons, you may want to trim the peel from the outer eggplant slices so they match the others. You can do the same thing with outer zucchini slices. Besides creating more attractive grill marks, the flesh cooks better when directly exposed to the heat.

Grilled Corn with Herb Butter

➤ **NOTE:** *Freshly picked sweet corn can be husked and then grilled directly over hot coals. Brush lightly with vegetable oil before grilling and then brush with herb butter just before serving. Serves four.*

3	tablespoons unsalted butter
2	tablespoons minced fresh parsley, thyme, cilantro, basil and/or other fresh herbs
	Salt and ground black pepper
4	ears of corn, husked
1	tablespoon vegetable oil

INSTRUCTIONS:

1. Build a single-level fire (*see* figure 3, page 15). Set grill rack in place, cover grill with lid, and let rack heat up, about 5 minutes.

2. Melt butter in small saucepan. Stir in herbs and salt and pepper to taste; keep butter warm.

3. Brush corn with vegetable oil. Grill corn, turning often, over medium fire, until kernels are lightly charred, about 4 minutes. Remove corn from grill, brush with herb butter and serve immediately.

Grilled Portobello Mushrooms, Red Pepper, and Garlic Croutons

➤ NOTE: *This grilled bread salad can be served as a side dish or even better as a first course for an outdoor grilled meal for four. The grilled croutons will become soggy fairly quickly. If you prepare this dish in advance, do not add them until just before serving.*

5   tablespoons extra-virgin olive oil

2   medium garlic cloves, minced

1   teaspoon grated zest and 1 tablespoon juice
    from medium lemon
    Salt and ground black pepper

2   large portobello mushrooms, cleaned with
    damp cloth and stems removed

1   large red bell pepper, cored, seeded, and cut
    into large wedges

4   1-inch-thick slices Italian bread

3   tablespoons minced fresh parsley leaves

⁞⁞ INSTRUCTIONS:

1. Build a single-level fire (*see* figure 3, page 15). Set grill rack in place, cover grill with lid, and let rack heat up, about 5 minutes.

2. Meanwhile, combine 4 tablespoons oil, garlic, lemon zest, and salt and pepper to taste in small bowl. Place mushrooms, red pepper, and bread slices on large platter; brush both sides of vegetables and bread with flavored oil.

3. Place vegetables and bread over medium-hot fire, making sure that gill-like undersides of mushrooms are facing up. Grill over medium-hot fire, turning pepper and bread once but leaving mushrooms as is, until vegetables and bread are streaked with dark grill marks, about 2 minutes for bread and 8 to 10 minutes for mushrooms and pepper.

4. Transfer grilled vegetables and bread to cutting board. Halve mushrooms, then cut into ½-inch-wide strips. Cut pepper into ¼-inch-wide strips. Cut bread into 1-inch croutons.

5. Toss vegetables in large serving bowl with remaining 1 tablespoon oil, lemon juice, and parsley. Adjust seasonings. (Vegetables can be covered and kept at room temperature for 1 hour.) Stir in croutons and serve immediately.

Grilled Asparagus with Almonds, Green Olives, and Sherry Vinaigrette

➤ NOTE: *Asparagus should be cooked on a cooler part of the grill to keep the tips from blackening. Serves four as a side dish.*

1	medium garlic clove, minced
½	teaspoon ground cumin
2	tablespoons chopped red onion
1	tablespoon sherry vinegar
2	tablespoons extra-virgin olive oil
	Salt and ground black pepper
1½	pounds asparagus, tough ends snapped off
¼	cup sliced almonds, toasted
2	tablespoons pitted and chopped green olives

INSTRUCTIONS:

1. Build a single-level fire (s*ee* figure 3, page 15). Set grill rack in place, cover grill with lid, and let rack heat up, about 5 minutes.

2. Combine garlic, cumin, onion, vinegar, oil, and salt and pepper to taste in small bowl. Place asparagus on platter and brush with 2 tablespoons dressing.

3. Lay asparagus spears perpendicular to the cooking grate so they won't fall onto the coals. Grill over medium fire, turning once, until streaked with light grill marks, 6 to 8 minutes. Transfer to serving dish and pour remaining dressing over grilled vegetables. Toss to coat, adjust seasonings, and scatter almonds and green olives on top. Serve hot or at room temperature.

■■ VARIATION:

Grilled Asparagus with Peanut Sauce

Combine following to make dressing: 1 minced garlic clove, 1 tablespoon Asian sesame oil, 1½ teaspoons each finely grated fresh gingerroot, rice wine vinegar, and soy sauce, and salt and pepper to taste. Brush 2 tablespoons dressing over asparagus before grilling. Stir 1 tablespoon each peanut butter, minced fresh cilantro leaves, and water into remaining dressing and pour over grilled asparagus. Garnish with 2 tablespoons chopped scallions.

index